IRON INTO FLOWER

poems by

Yvette Neisser

Finishing Line Press
Georgetown, Kentucky

IRON INTO FLOWER

Copyright © 2022 by Yvette Neisser
ISBN 979-8-88838-003-1 First Edition
All rights reserved under International and Pan-American Copyright Conventions. No part of this book may be reproduced in any manner whatsoever without written permission from the publisher, except in the case of brief quotations embodied in critical articles and reviews.

Publisher: Leah Huete de Maines
Editor: Christen Kincaid
Cover Art: Yvette Neisser
Author Photo: Mark Kokkoros
Cover Design: Elizabeth Maines McCleavy

Order online: www.finishinglinepress.com
also available on amazon.com

Author inquiries and mail orders:
Finishing Line Press
P. O. Box 1626
Georgetown, Kentucky 40324
U. S. A.

Table of Contents

I. THE ARC OF THE SUN
THE ARC OF THE SUN 1
TEA 2
COMPASS POINTS 4
GRAVITY 5
SLOW 6
HORIZON 8

II. NONFICTION
PORTRAIT WITH LEAVES 13
REVISIONIST HISTORY 15
NONFICTION 16
DAYENU 18
SO THIS IS HOW THEY DECIDED TO TAKE HIM 20
THE SHAPE OF FAITH 21
THE WHOLE IMPERFECT LOT OF US 22

III. ECHOES
YVETTE 27
HOW LOVE BEGINS 28
BECOMING LATINA 29
SPARK 30
ECHOES 31
LETTER FOR THE NEW YEAR 33
LET ME TELL YOU A SECRET 34
HUSBAND 35
FOR A MARRIAGE 36
OCTOBER EVENING 37
AIR TRAVEL 38
MOVING 39

IV. SEASON OF GRIEF

WHAT YOU LEFT BEHIND 45
SEASON OF GRIEF 46
BLAZE 48
THE SAME LIFE 49
SEASON OF HUNGER 50
LEARNING TO LOVE MORNING 51
MANTRA TO GET THROUGH JANUARY 52
MANTRA TO GET OUT OF DEPRESSION 53
PRAYING MANTIS 54

V. IRON INTO FLOWER

NEISSER 59
DECLARATION OF INDEPENDENCE FROM MY
     FORMER SELF 60
LATE APRIL 62
BEFORE SUNRISE 63
ONE LIGHT 64
SPRING IS RIOTOUS 65
THE SILENCE AFTER THE PERFORMANCE 66
YOSHINO CHERRY 67
PASSION 68
TEXTURE 69

NOTES 70

ACKNOWLEDGEMENTS 71

I. THE ARC OF THE SUN

THE ARC OF THE SUN

for my mother

Here is what you have revealed: At eighteen,
you rode a Greyhound from New Jersey
all the way down to the border and beyond,
into Mexico, where you spent a summer
wrapped in a novio's serenades and
the tortillas of a kind family.
You say you don't remember the rest.
But there are some things I know.
It was 1965, you were
a young woman breaking out
from the shelter of aunts and uncles,
from kugels and Yiddish jokes, to take
the only route to Mexico:
three days through the Deep South, where
segregation was shaking at the seams,
separate water fountains smashed
to pieces. Remember, the South was heaving,
"colored only" signs yanked from walls,
Jews considered a separate race.
Buses cranked nervously through states
where Freedom Riders were torched and beaten.
Were you ever afraid? You deny memory
and live only in the present,
placing your faith in the arc of the sun
at each hour. Whatever happened that summer,
you came home with the private tongue
of Spanish, a pocketful of tales
you could tell, but chose not to.
Maybe the ride back was easier,
reversing the journey from South to North.
Maybe you were no longer white,
having absorbed the Aztec sun.
Maybe you had shed fear.

TEA

in memory of my grandmother Sylvia

Served black with sugar
at my grandmother's house,
it opened the door
to the secret world of grown-ups,
letting us in to a dark sweetness,
letting us open the drawer
under the china cabinet
to take out the playing cards,
each deck with its own story
of Pinochle or a long-gone uncle.

Consumed upon entering any home
or departing, upon arising
and before lying down,
with plum cake or pistachios,
a crossword or the evening news,
or chocolates from the glass dish
that never ran empty.

Never replaced with coffee or wine,
never iced or infused with raspberry.

Never brewed with loose leaves
that might sink to the bottom
and tell our futures,
never herbal or chai,
never diluted with milk,
never served in anything
but teacup and saucer.

Just boil water on the stove,
pour it over a fiber bag
with tea leaves stapled inside
and a tag hanging by a string.

Let the cup have an angled rim.
Let it be white and shaped like petals,
the handle small enough
to hold with three fingers.

Let color seep into hot water,
let steam rise into memory.

Drink it Lipton. Drink it black.

COMPASS POINTS

in memory of my father

This is our history: we'd enter the woods,
step into pine needles, mud, asters,
fallen leaves—and there among the trunks
and weaving spiders, we built our love
on the shoulders of the giving earth.

I stumbled into adulthood,
veering from crevice to crevice,
scraping for my own space,
observing violet petals while you asked
the hard questions: why this boyfriend,
why quit this job, why pick up your life
from this city and plant it in another?

You'd sprint as we neared the peak,
impatient to see the view from every angle,
to identify our compass points,
to find the perfect landmark.

I preferred the climb,
discovering detours and hidden nooks,
exploring every path.

Still, we both loved to look
for sunlight above the tree line,
to ponder a certain rock
or fallen trunk ringed with time,
as the years have etched rings around my life,
first with you, then without you.

GRAVITY

Somewhere on the outskirts
of Santa Cruz, down a side road
out of town, gravity is reversed.

I'm not making this up.

In someone's backyard,
all we knew to be true
was turned upside down:
put a metal ball
at the bottom of a ramp,
and it rolled up.

What magnets hung
in the air—or magic—
to make every object tilt upwards,
gravity now pulling everything
toward the sky?

I believed it all.
I still do.

Every road home somehow bent
toward Lombard Street,
the red snake curve, wheels rolling
over each brick, and our father would say
I think I'll comb my hair
and take his hands off the wheel
as my sister and I shrieked in the back seat

and the world opened up, didn't it—
sunshine, baskets of flowers
pouring out their colors
at every turn,
the road twisting and twisting.

SLOW

Consider the pace of the seasons

how the sun sets just a touch later each day
until arriving at spring

how a heron wades into water
each reedy step balancing in mud

the pull of oars up a quiet river
the ripples

the meander through wildflowers
the sundial and its shadows

the mulling of cider
the steeping of tea

how rice absorbs water
and aloe seeps into skin

consider things made by hand

the stitching the weaving
mosaics glued piece by piece

grandfather clocks and church bells
rung every hour with a rope

lighthouses lit by a keeper
conversations that go deep

music played on a single instrument
the pluck of strings
the human voice

the linger
the pause

the long bath
the cleanse of pores
fingers through each curl of hair

the complete breath
filling the belly
the lungs and then

holding an *asana*
pressing each finger down
the lift of hips

rotation of shoulders
stretch of muscle
fiber by fiber

the exhale
the closing of eyelids
the stillness

HORIZON

for Flavia d'Cunha, in memoriam

You hold a cup of coffee,
still waking up. The sun

just brimming over the horizon
with all its morning fury,

then suddenly huge and brilliant,
casting a glare over these streets

so even the pavement
and the leaves of every tree

become white fire, the edges
of traffic lights so crisply clear

they shock your eyes.
So ordinary, so harsh.

That's when you
step off the curb

into another day,
towards the tiny beacon

of a lone bus sign
staked on a corner,

and enter the white fire burning
in the eyes of one driver—

then make contact with asphalt,
that tarred surface

between us
and the vulnerable earth.

II. NONFICTION

Call of muezzin.
Open window, winter chill.
The eye of a crow.

PORTRAIT WITH LEAVES

*After the photograph ¿Sólo una sombra? Only a Shadow? (Ester IV)
by Muriel Hasbun, 1993-94*

i

What is it about her face
that says *Poland*

a sealed smile
lips upturned
eyes closed as if imagining

light falls from above
casting her in a halo

the leaves in the foreground
crisp   almost palpable
whitened by the sun or the lens

ii

Is it a window behind her
are the blinds open or shut

they tantalize with open spaces
between each slat

like the barbed wire fence
at Auschwitz dividing Jews
from the world outside

so close to freedom
you could breathe it
through the gaps

iii

Was it all a dream

the bodies long burned
ashes long cleaned
furnaces long cold

is it all in her head now
can she blank it out
like my grandmother
who disappeared each afternoon
into the back bedroom
with a secret mantra
that might sound like *ohm*

iv

She is at home with leaves

how each human life is like a leaf

how a spirit alive and singing
in a moment becomes a body

another corpse
how easily a person can let go

v

Is it so far gone now
that she can float in these leaves?

REVISIONIST HISTORY

In a world without Hitler,
the synagogues could still be standing,
still filling with worshippers
on Shabbat mornings. My grandfather
could have stayed in Germany,

the great house in Frankfurt
could still belong to our family.
My father could have grown up there,
sliding down the wooden banisters,
listening to piano symphonies
float up from the music room.

Gas chambers never invented.
Dachau, a nice place to visit.
My aunt's first word, not *Achtung*.
"After the war" not the line
demarking the moment
when my grandmother
refused to speak German.

I could have read Rilke in the original.
People would be able to spell my names.

NONFICTION

i

I didn't want this poem.
No one wanted a poem like this.

From my grandmother
came down a legacy—
the words *concentration camp*,
the word *holocaust*—
and every piece of history,
every *Achtung*, every aria sung
in a barrack, rising into the night
to slake her parched dreams,
every call of "Never Again"
became mine, a coat of arms
I have carried all my life.

Have I borne it well?
Should I wield it
or hide behind it?

ii

March 2012. Homs, Syria.
The headline reads:
women and children
stabbed
        burned to death

iii

In the president's quarters,
Bashar al-Assad
just wants a cup of coffee.

It's not easy, you know,
clamping the lid
on the revolution.

You have to keep pressing it down
until the women shut up
and the babies stop crying,

until no one survives but you,
and you step outside
to walk among the remains:

a landscape barren of flower,
smoke still brimming
from the angry bones.

DAYENU

May 2021

Had God taken us out of Europe alive,
it would have been enough.

Had He taken us out of Europe alive
and brought us into the land of Israel,
it would have been enough.

Had we entered the land of Israel
and revived the Hebrew language,
carving its letters on ruins and gravestones,
renaming cities and villages,
it would have been enough.

Had we renamed cities and villages
while Arabic was covered in dust,
enough.

Had we built settlements
but not checkpoints

Had we claimed Jerusalem
but not evicted its residents

Had we evicted them
but not dragged them from their homes

Had we controlled the Old City
but not raided al-Aqsa

not disrupted Ramadan prayers,
Iftar meals, Eid celebrations

Had we occupied Gaza
but not shut off the borders—

Had we shut off the borders
but not bombed homes—

Had we bombed homes for one day
but not for days on end—
it would have been enough.

I swear it would have been enough.

SO THIS IS HOW THEY DECIDED TO TAKE HIM

Mexico City, 2013

So this is how they decided to take him—
at the end of his life,
his frame shrunken, his wild rambling days over,
his days of bar fights and women over—
they waited until now,
at eighty years old,
when he had no strength to fight—
snatched him off the street,
gagged him and bundled him into a car
with darkened windows.

He, a fifty-year citizen of Mexico,
Spanish rolling off his tongue,
lashing his takers with curses
in their own language.

In the end, they took him
like a sack of meat,
threw him in the car,
and finally, after calling his family
and extorting all the money they could—
not much—
after stripping him of every dollar
and every belonging on his body,
they did unto their elder
the only thing they knew—
bestowed him with a bullet.

THE SHAPE OF FAITH

Rosh Hashanah, 1998/5759

All rise—the opening of the ark.
The congregation rustles to its feet,
tassels of tallit sway with mumbled prayers
and I ask God, *are you somewhere?*

Sunlight skims the surface of the room,
radiating across the sanctuary,
refracted in eyeglasses and the shine
of polished wood, illumining cylinders of air.

But when I lift my hand
to touch them, the shapes fragment
into particles, hovering and lit.

The rabbi moves into the congregation
as into a sea of reeds, pausing at each step,
as people bend with outstretched prayer books
to touch the Torah in his arms.

Above the ark's wooden doors, brass letters
gleam with their own certainty:
Da lifnei mi atah omed
"Know before whom you stand."

And close to the ceiling
in the circle of a brass lamp,
a wavering flame always burns.

From this, can I learn
the shape of faith? A tear
flickering and turning,
blue into orange, contours
shifting, narrowing
to a single point of light.

THE WHOLE IMPERFECT LOT OF US

Yom Kippur, 2010

You must change your life,
say the rabbis of old.
Shine a mirror inside yourselves,
examine your flaws.
Scrub the soul clean.

As we sit in silence,
one boy cannot control his voice.
Now and then he lets out a howl,
shaking us out of contemplation.

Bless him for digging deep.

Bless us all, the whole imperfect lot of us—
the ones with hair combed neatly
      and those with unruly hair
the ones who stand still in prayer
      and those who shuffle from foot to foot
the ones who pray aloud
      and those who read silently
the ones who mutter the words
      and those who simply hum the tune
the ones with eyes fixed on the prayer book
      and those whose eyes wander the room.

Bless the boy whose voice awakens us
      and those who look away.

III. ECHOES

*A flash of lightning
frames your face in silhouette.
Birds chirp in the dark.*

YVETTE

This name derived from the yew tree
and given to me in 1973
for my mother's love of French
and a *Boricua* girl with black braids,
my father's favorite student
when he taught second grade,
his refuge from the draft,
when they lived in one room
and a hamper served as his desk.

A name that has passed through languages,
from Germanic into French,
linking me in a chain from Saint Yves
to the girl with Spanish twined in her hair,
to my own brown curls.

This name I carry, reminder
of a time long forgotten
in our American family,
where English came to dominate,
pushing Yiddish and German
into the distant sphere of grandparents,
Spanish and French into the eaves
of my parents' youth.

Yvette, written with a Y
that sounds like an E,
mispronounced all my life,
its first syllable a mystery vowel
on the tongues of friends and teachers.

Who knew the language of the braids
would find its way back,
that one day I would find Neruda
and grow into Spanish.
It is in me. I contain it.

HOW LOVE BEGINS

A pure blue,
the color of ocean.

His voice, always
singing, whistling.

Waves lap in,
fronds of ferns lengthen,

wisteria winds around trees.
A rush of colors:

red of tomato and deep green
of serranos, simmer of onion.

Cumbia and serenades.
Friction of skin. Learning

which scent arouses,
which fabric entices.

Honeymoon of waterfalls,
pine forests and lingerie.

Metal blue of midnight
into the inkling of day.

Fingers on fingers,
palm to palm. How it feels

to have your hand in his,
now, maybe forever.

BECOMING LATINA

Was it when I claimed
my own last name—Moreno—
leaning on the r, turning it hard
over my tongue—this name,
meaning dark-skinned,
meaning the color of the Moors
who inhabited Spain centuries ago;
this name that my husband inherited
from a father he never knew?

Or was it over the stove
when my fingers learned
to flip the tortillas
without getting burned?

Was it between the pen
and the paper? In the margin
between the Spanish and the English?
When the subjunctive untangled
from the reflexive, the imperfect
from the preterite, the *usted* from the *tú*?

Did the language flow down
from my tongue into my body,
or did a tremor of salsa enter my hips
and speak through my tongue?
Did verb endings enter my dreams
and filter through my limbs?

If you fall deep enough
into your lover's eyes
and allow yourself to dwell there,
fumbling around until you feel
the contours of a world called *Mexico*,
until finally you can lean back
and the mesh is there to catch you,
and it feels like home—
does that make you Latina?

SPARK

From love,
from a spark of desire,
an egg nestles in the lining of my womb.

How does a tiny mass of cells
become this heartbreaking creature,
a full-bodied human,

her four-chambered heart
beating at the side of my womb
when I lie down and when I rise up?

She blooms from my body
to breathe on my skin, lulled
by the thump of my heart.

ECHOES

after W.S. Merwin's The Folding Cliffs

We keep close to the house

Sometimes when we are alone
it's not enough for you to sit by my side

Though there's nothing to frighten you
no rain or darkness or flashes of light

> still you climb into my lap
> and together we hold the toy bus
> turn the wheels around

When you sleep I read about Kauai
enter thickets forests winter rains

> its place names flow into me
> and I move through the day
> humming Kalalau Kalalau

Your cry too has permeated me
so even when I'm far
I hear its timbre
as in the rush of water

In my slumber it all blends together
my life the seaside cliffs
the murmur of streams

This morning
awakened by your sharp cry
I ran to cradle you
but your room was quiet

> just my subconscious
> echoing your cry inside my dream

Outside the sun had not risen
but the sky was lightening
soft blue with strips of white
above the pines

I climbed into bed with your father
warmed myself against his body
still heavy with sleep
listened to his breathing
and closed my eyes to imagine

        how the white would now
        brighten with sun and then

the whole sky would light up

LETTER FOR THE NEW YEAR

Chinese New Year, February 2005

Just when you pointed to the snow
finally melting off the deck
and a cardinal perched there
like a harbinger of spring,
flakes again began to fall,
edging the pine needles in white.

Winter is upon us, and you are sprouting
words and numbers, counting to 100,
announcing "B for bus" and "T for train";
you reach light switches, refuse to sleep,
empty your plate onto the table.

This is the year of the rooster. A year of luck.
Our neighbors prepare a whole chicken for breakfast.

This year we discovered
that you like snow only after it's fallen;
you shudder from the wet shock
of flakes touching your face.

And a group of deer
has taken to bedding down
in the woods behind the house.
When I approach, they do not flee.
I take this as a sign of luck.

LET ME TELL YOU A SECRET

On the second floor of an ordinary house,
there is a closed door. Behind it,
early in the morning, a little girl
is taking a bath.

While the neighbors are asleep
or drinking their coffee,
she watches the play of light
on the metal faucet, the magic of water
running over her fingers.

How light and water
create their own world,
a tapestry across the surface.
Here, a child has discovered
a pure, transparent joy.

HUSBAND

A hand
that reaches out

mooring me
from a night of wind-tossed dreams

luring me back to port
this bed our *terra firma*

the heat of his palm
the only thing that holds me here

like the weight that keeps a tarp
from flying into the storm

FOR A MARRIAGE

for Shira and Ron

Sometimes you have to wait a while.
You may have to forge river bottoms
      or tunnel through mountains
before love is ready to come.
You may have to dig
into the contours of your soul,
traverse the world and back.

Love comes when it will.
It may catch you from behind
or seep into your life
like water into soil.

Sometimes love opens like a blossom in your hands.

Let it be the fire that starts you in the morning
and the breeze that cools you at night.
Let it be a fountain that nourishes you,
the earthstone that cushions your steps.

May love mingle with prayer
and propel you toward kindness.

Take this love, twine it as a rope
between your hands.
May it sanctify you.
May it be a ballast to your days.

OCTOBER EVENING

Darkness comes early
and surrounds us
like a tent closing its canvas.

In the glow of kitchen light,
my children's faces
are all that matter.

AIR TRAVEL

From the journey
only this is real:

sunset over the peaks
the shimmer of the bay

your presence next to me
as Maryland rises up
to the plane window

beauty is what matters
the sun's descent
highlighting the mountains'
contours in pink

is this love I wonder
you and I side by side
as the plane hums over the landscape

Maryland's waters tilt
and seem to recognize us

your eyes are what I know

if only I had more than words
if this ache inside me
could rise like a cloud
and form a shape wide enough
for all my colors

MOVING

Wind blasts into dawn
the earth senses my trembling
pear blossoms scatter

      spring chill hearkens change
      these walls these closets
      will be emptied of memories

this haiku is yet to be finished

IV. SEASON OF GRIEF

Red to maroon, orange to rust.
Green deepens,
softens with the sky.

WHAT YOU LEFT BEHIND

after a marriage

A closet full of tools
I cannot name.
An industrial-strength vacuum.
Receipts from 2005.
Books you never read.

A 40-foot ladder.
Empty, crusted paint cans.

Years of dust in the corners
we never swept.
Cracked window sills and peeling paint.
Curtains hung crookedly.
Others never hung.

The bed we bought together.
And the sheets we slept on.
How many years.

Dreams where I sense you
lying next to me
and wake up
saying no, no, no.

Your last name
on every document I own.
The hollow of its vowels.

SEASON OF GRIEF

Autumn 2016

This is the season.
Let us grieve all our losses. Grieve
the timidity of youth,
our first loves. All the sunsets
we missed, those heavy suns
sinking beyond the cusp.

Grieve the places we haven't been.
They are stunning. So vast the sky,
so deep the water's reflection.

And the poems not written,
the ones that sank
into the night
as you fell into dream.

Grieve your father.
He always leaves you in this season,
year after year, bequeathing the final notes
of Eine Kleine Nachtmusik

and the long leaves of a corn plant
curving in pairs dark green,
reaching to the ceiling.

Grieve your body,
all the places it sags,
the aches and crannies.

Grieve the loss of color
as orange and red cascade
and crumble into brown,
then earth,
then bareness.

Grieve the days shortening,
the sacrifice of light
to the other side of the world.

Let go
as the trees do
loosening hold on the stem
of each leaf
until they float into the air
weightless.

BLAZE

Sunrise, January 1, 2017

2016 began with heartbreak
and ended with a stepfather's leukemia.

In between was the darkest hole
in which I dwelled and shriveled.
Pounds fell off,
hair thinned and flattened,
skin paled, clothes hung
on shapeless hips and breasts.

Every day I was afraid.
Summer sun blazed morning
through curtains, and I craved
darkness. The bed a refuge.

I forgot words and appointments,
school papers and friends' birthdays,
how to make jokes
and thread words into poems.

Meanwhile, his blood cells caved
to the disease, first the red ones,
then the platelets. Then the bacteria came,
coursing through his marrow.

As the year turns, we brace
for winter and gradual weakening.
I dig in for strength.

THE SAME LIFE

Here in my kitchen-haven-prison
glass separates me from the sunset
from the greenery of pines and poplars

Here this bed where I dream
traveling through countries
through lovers past and imagined

I wake up to the same life
the ceiling and its edges
shadows in each corner
doorknobs still brass
and attached with screws

Nothing has fallen apart
except my soul crumbling inside my body

If I could hold something in my hand
a fluttering moth
alive and pulsing
or a fig just plucked from the stem

SEASON OF HUNGER

Winter 2017

Every day is shocking.
The wind lashes colder,

our new president
slashes another agency,

my appetite rages,
hungry for everything.

I am learning tryptophan and iodide,
yoga and the seven chakras,
how they infuse body and mind.

Temperatures drop,
the body stiffens and aches,
everything leaks, the roof gives in.

I learn how to stand again,
how to breathe, how to hold my body:
shoulder blades, ribs, pelvis.

My feet had forgotten
how to grip the earth,
my voice how to speak.

LEARNING TO LOVE MORNING

Night always lured me
the stars the mystery
the fading of colors
the hush and deep

Now night calls for sleep
as the sky darkens through curtains
it is dawn that calls
and rouses me to the woods

Morning has its own mysteries
sometimes the stars are out
before their flight across hemispheres
grass is covered in dew or mist

houses are dark
the air is crisp

poplar and maple leaves
have yet to unfurl

their trunks still hold the secrets of night
whatever arbolean dreams they stored

there's the rustle of squirrels
and deer grazing in shadow

all is pale and soft

then the sharp call of morning birds

one day I vow to learn their names

MANTRA TO GET THROUGH JANUARY

Winter pull me in
        to your luster of snow
how it cushions the world
        and nurtures the soil

lay me in sodden grass
        frozen and raw
a touch of green
        in the pale season

give me the drip of icicles
        drag my fingers
along their shapes
        smooth and sharp

pull me under the surface
        where frogs hibernate in ponds
flowers hide in their seeds
        and insects do their winter thing

give me back the sensations
        flakes wet on my face
wind slipping under my scarf
        the slide of ice the seep of mud

let me not hide
        let me feel it

winter
        shake me alive

MANTRA TO GET OUT OF DEPRESSION

Remember the stars
rushing water
a bird's cry

fresh breeze
and raspberries

feeling luscious
in a bath or silk blouse

remember what is tactile
a cut amethyst
lamb's ear
the pages of a book
between your fingers

remember sunshine or shade
in a hollow
how wood is carved
how words transfer
from one language to another

how roses bloom in the heat
and emit their scents
each a different shade of sweet

were I a rose
were I a heron
standing in the river

PRAYING MANTIS

for Dottie May, in memoriam

I should have known
when the magnolias died in frost,
it would be her last spring—
the way the blossoms hung on for weeks,
brown and wilted, shrouding the house
with their flitting petal shadows.

She had taken to wandering the yard
as if surveying the inches of grass
and patches of garden, each flowering plant
she had tended these fifty years. She no longer
called to me across the fence
to show me something of beauty—
a budding hydrangea, a ripening fig

or a praying mantis
crouched among daffodils,
perched on forelegs,
alert to whatever comes next.

V. IRON INTO FLOWER

*The sky holds daylight
into evening. When dawn comes
I will shed my skin.*

NEISSER

This name I have carried all my life.
From a river dividing two countries,
from the Polish border to the great house
in Frankfurt, and then to America.
How a surname carries the substance
of lineage, how it embodies my grandfather:
Gerhardt, Jerry, man of cello and linguae.

This name, stifled for years
between Yvette and Moreno.
How I want to put it in stars,
bolded letters, all caps.

I bring this name out of hiding,
bring it back to the fore,

I take Neisser to be my beloved name,
in love and anger, sickness and health,

stamp this name on my back
and bind it to my doorposts,

take this name to be my core,
my rock and my redeemer.

Submerged in living waters,
alone in my skin,

I shed the letters of marriage
and watch them float away.

DECLARATION OF INDEPENDENCE FROM MY FORMER SELF

I lost everything:
the contours of the body I knew
the house
the identity of wife/mother
half of a couple
a name that began with Mrs.

Everything I thought I held dear
came apart, unhinged
from their places:
the photo albums
the arrangement of furniture
the banisters that connected
one floor to the next

the days defined by children's routines
school buses in the morning
stories in the evening

When I walked out in the world
a ring bound my finger
declaring my status

but I am not bound
I am a fireball
shooting sparks

I am light and dark
rainbow and shadow
fuchsia and turquoise

dancer and explorer
vessel for languages
archaeologist of feelings

I declare freedom
unlock the gate to the world
fling the door open

mother and wanderer
mother and sky
mother and wild
mother and expanse
mother and let it all in

LATE APRIL

Trees into bloom
  the scent of pollen
    heavy with seed

windows shut all winter
  are raised from their sills
    curtains parted

spring breaks open
  and we want the rush
    wind through sunlight

the promise of color at dawn
  twig into leaf
    dew on petals

the mourning dove
  calling us to worship

we are joy
we are sorrow

we are song and flutter

we are the nests building

we are hooves through wet earth

we are mortar and buds

BEFORE SUNRISE

Seattle, 2015

Sleep eludes me
what I know is how to be awake

how to tread these streets
like a shadow

I surprise even the mountains

still emerging from the clouds
defining their shapes

I've forgotten the outside world

it's just me and the evergreens
and the scent of pink magnolias

I have caught the sun
which came when I beckoned

Shall I be reborn here
among the pine?

ONE LIGHT

Those hollow hours
in the small of the night:
a narrow valley of wakefulness
between two steep cliffs.

I am the camera left out with the lens open,
the one light in a dark house,
the reflection of moonlight
in a still pond.

SPRING IS RIOTOUS

Moths flutter into windows,
cherry blossoms swirl and fall,
pollen blows on every surface,
my azaleas unfurl.

In this, I awaken. In this,
my flower opens,
wet and wondrous.
Rifts let me in.

THE SILENCE AFTER THE PERFORMANCE

for Julian Wachner, former conductor of The Washington Chorus

When the conductor lowers his hands
        from crescendo
        to utter silence
        arms tensed
        fingers towards the floor

When the singer is motionless
        neck arched with the tilt
        of her last note

an orchestra in still life
so many bodies
straining against the instinct
        to shiver or shudder

now the conductor's reach
extends from his fingertips
        to the very last row of seats
and the audience obeys this gesture
this ultimate un-notated rest
this convergence of chorus and audience
        when two silences meet

YOSHINO CHERRY

after María Teresa Ogliastri

You'd think nothing could penetrate
that bark, silvered and solid as a wall—

yet flowers burst
straight from the trunk:

first a tiny shoot,
a spray of buds,
then bouquets of blossoms.

These petals,
translucent to the touch,
veined and edged in pink.

Cherry tree, show me
how to draw beauty
from the rough spots,
how surfaces can shift—
iron into flower,
stasis into flux.

PASSION

Let it be deep

send fire to the sun
      water to the sea

slake the arid places
      calm the rumbling

bring back my voice
      my heart to my body

TEXTURE

Hungry for color, for touch.
        For the rough skin of nuts
                and the sweetness of pear.

For the wildness
        of wild animals, raw
                and gritty, teeth and dirt.

For sticky summer heat,
        groove and clutch,
                lick and steep.

For the opening of flowers,
        the complete softness of petals.
                How they turn their insides out,

their deepest colors in every shade.
        When they are ready,
                nothing is hidden.

Could I be that brazen,
        that vulnerable. Could I be
                that soft all the time.

NOTES

Gravity: The place described in this poem is known as "The Mystery Spot."

Slow: An *asana* (Sanskrit) is a yoga pose.

Horizon: Flavia D'Cunha was a young mother who was hit by a car and killed in the author's neighborhood in Silver Spring, Maryland, circa 2008.

Nonfiction / Revisionist History: *Achtung*, German for "attention," is what Nazi soldiers would shout upon walking into a barracks, according to the author's grandmother.

Dayenu: This poem is a play on the traditional Passover song, "Dayenu," meaning "enough," or, literally, "enough for us." The song expresses gratitude for God's generosity in bringing the Jews out of slavery in Egypt.
> "…If God had brought us out of Egypt but not given us the Torah, it would have been enough. *Dayenu*
> If He had given us the Torah but not given us the Sabbath, it would have been enough. *Dayenu*
> If he had given us the Sabbath but not brought us into the land of Israel, it would have been enough. *Dayenu*"

Al-Aqsa Mosque in Jerusalem's Old City (also known as the Dome of the Rock) is the third holiest site in Islam; it sits atop the Western Wall, the holiest site in Judaism. *Iftar* is the evening meal shared by families after the daily fast during Ramadan.

So This Is How They Decided to Take Him: Kidnapping is an "epidemic" in Mexico, a common way for criminal gangs—often drug traffickers—to extort money from their victims (https://www.vox.com/2018/5/11/17276638/mexico-kidnappings-crime-cartels-drug-trade). Sometimes victims are released after the ransom money is received, but often the victims are killed or "disappeared." This poem tells the true story of one tragic victim, an elderly American expat.

Neisser: The phrase "bind it to my doorposts" echoes Deuteronomy 6, part of the core Jewish liturgy recited during weekly Sabbath services. "Living waters" refers to a *mikvah*, a Jewish ritual bath.

ACKNOWLEDGEMENTS

Grateful acknowledgement is made to the editors of the following publications, where some of these poems first appeared, often in earlier versions:

ArLiJo: "Letter for the New Year," "The Whole Imperfect Lot of Us"

Beltway Poetry Quarterly: "Revisionist History" (reprinted from *MiPoesias*)

Bourgeon: "Husband," "What You Left Behind," "Yvette," "Declaration of Independence from My Former Self," "The Arc of the Sun," "Gravity," and "Texture"

District Lit: "Compass Points," "Praying Mantis"

Literal: "Becoming Latina"

MiPoesias: "Revisionist History"

Peacock Journal: "Horizon" (published as "For Flavia D'Cunha, in Memoriam"), "For a Marriage," "Learning to Love Morning," "Mantra to Get through January," "Neisser," "Tea," and "Yoshino Cherry"

Poet Lore: "Portrait with Leaves"

The Quarry: A Social Justice Poetry Database (https://www.splitthisrock.org/poetry-database): "So This is How They Decided to Take Him"

Sligo Journal: "Slow"

Tikkun: "Dayenu"

Anthologies:

The Bloomsbury Anthology of Contemporary American Poetry, ed. Nancy Naomi Carlson and Matthew Silverman. New York: Bloomsbury Press, 2013: "The Shape of Faith."

101 Jewish Poems for the Third Millennium, ed. Matthew E. Silverman and Nancy Naomi Carlson. Ashland, Ohio: Ashland Poetry Press, 2021: "The Whole Imperfect Lot of Us."

The Great World of Days, ed. Gregory Luce, Anne Becker, and Jeffrey Banks. Washington, DC: Day Eight, 2022: "What You Left Behind."

I also would like to thank the many people who provided valuable feedback on this manuscript or individual poems: Lavonne Adams, Naomi Ayala, Elana Bell, Michael Brendzel (in memoriam), Sarah Browning, Jessie Handforth Kome, Alan Loeb, Carrie Noel-Nossbaum, Lucia Pires.

Yvette Neisser is the author of *Grip,* winner of the 2011 Gival Poetry Prize. Founder of the DC-Area Literary Translators Network (DC-ALT), her translations from Spanish include *South Pole/Polo Sur* by María Teresa Ogliastri and *Difficult Beauty: Selected Poems* by Luis Alberto Ambroggio. She also contributed to the anthology *Knocking on the Door of the White House: Latino and Latina Poets of Washington, D.C.*

Yvette has taught creative writing, poetry translation, and literature at numerous institutions, including The George Washington University, Catholic University, and The Writer's Center (Bethesda, MD). She has lectured on translation at venues such as the Library of Congress, the Embassy of Argentina, and Georgetown University. For several years, she was a roving "poet in the schools" at public schools in Maryland, Virginia, and Washington, DC.

Her passion for international affairs and cultures has been a driving force not only in her writing but also in her professional career. After studying in Egypt and Israel, her work in international development and research has taken her to Africa, the Middle East, South America, and Europe.

Originally from New Jersey, she lives in Silver Spring, Maryland, just outside of Washington, DC.

www.ingramcontent.com/pod-product-compliance
Lightning Source LLC
Chambersburg PA
CBHW030224170426
43194CB00007BA/855